Starting with the Old Testament

A Lion First Guide

Starting with the
Old Testament

STEPHEN TRAVIS

A LION BOOK

Text copyright © 1994 Stephen Travis
Illustrations and maps copyright © 1994 Tony de Saulles
This edition copyright © 1994 Lion Publishing

The author asserts the moral right
to be identified as the author of this work

Published by
Lion Publishing plc
Sandy Lane West, Oxford, England
ISBN 0 7459 3001 8
Albatross Books Pty Ltd
PO Box 320, Sutherland, NSW 2232, Australia
ISBN 0 7324 0849 0

First edition 1994

Acknowledgments
All Scripture quotations in this publication are from the
HOLY BIBLE, NEW INTERNATIONAL VERSION.
Copyright © 1973, 1978, 1984 by International Bible
Society. Used by permission.

Picture acknowledgments
Illustrations and maps by Tony de Saulles
Photographs by Lion Publishing 39, (David Alexander)
16, 24, 54, 55 (British Museum), (David Townsend) 3;
Hutchison Library 29; Skjold Photography 7 (all);
ZEFA 14, 61

A catalogue record for this book is available
from the British Library

Printed and bound in Singapore

Contents

1

What's in the Old Testament for us?

● ● ● ● ● ● ● ● ● ● ● ● ●

'I never knew such a God existed.' The speaker taught chemistry in an Indian university. He had grown up in one of India's oppressed groups, despised and exploited by higher social classes. Determined to get his own back on those who oppressed him and his community, he threw himself into his education and went to college committed to the revolutionary ideals of Marxism.

At college he was given a Bible by some Christian students and read it out of casual interest. There in the Old Testament he discovered a God who constantly takes the side of the poor against their oppressors; a God who cared enough about the everyday lives of ordinary people to make laws about their safety, laws to protect them against being bullied by the rich and powerful; a God who is just and expects justice among the people he has created.

'I never knew such a God existed,' he said. But he also read—still in the Old Testament—of a God who forgives, a God 'slow to anger and abounding in love and faithfulness'.

He found that harder to take. 'I was attracted to the God of justice and holiness. I ran away from a God of love.' But the God of love couldn't let him go. Christian friends explained more of how God's love reaches us through Jesus Christ. And he experienced for himself the love of the God whom he had met in the pages of the Old Testament.

The Old Testament isn't just an old book full of do's and don'ts. It isn't a collection of fairy stories. Old it certainly is. But it still speaks to questions which people face today:

◆ Why was the world made?

◆ Why do innocent people suffer?

◆ How are we meant to care for each other in society?

◆ Is history just a meaningless sequence of events, or is it going somewhere?

◆ Will God listen to my anger, my doubts, my questions as well as to my worship?

The Old Testament isn't just a book full of do's and don'ts. It still speaks to questions which people face today.

Is the Old Testament still relevant today?

People often assume that because the Old Testament is old it no longer has value. An old painting may be worth millions. A truth discovered long ago—for example, the truth that the earth goes round the sun—is as true today as when it was first discovered. But an old book, we tend to think, belongs to a bygone age. It cannot speak to a world of nuclear power and genetic engineering.

Can the Old Testament be relevant in a world of nuclear power and genetic engineering?

And Christians who value the New Testament are inclined to dismiss the Old Testament as inferior and no longer necessary. After all, it was Christians who took the Hebrew scriptures and called them the 'Old Testament', implying that they now had something better.

But there are strong reasons why the Old Testament should not be dismissed so easily.

◆ **Though the Old Testament doesn't deal with many of the specific issues of modern life, the really important things about human nature remain the same now as then.**

The Old Testament deals with the great issues of our experience—the contradictions between good and evil within us, the use and abuse of power, our longing for security and for a better world, our grappling with doubt and suffering, our search for shape and purpose in our lives.

◆ **To ignore it is to undervalue the great contribution of the Jewish people to human wisdom and our understanding of God.**

The legal systems of much of the world depend on the foundation of the Ten Commandments, and the Old Testament images of God, for example as the good shepherd, have spread far beyond their original settings in Palestine.

◆ **From a Christian viewpoint, the Old Testament belongs with the New, as the two acts of a two-act play belong together.**

Much of the important action occurs in Act Two. But if you don't see Act One you can't understand how the events of Act Two are significant. The Old Testament tells a story which points forward to the coming of the Messiah; the New Testament tells how the Messiah came and what he can mean for the whole world. And Jesus himself showed a thorough knowledge of the Old Testament.

◆ **The New Testament doesn't ignore the Old Testament but builds on it.**

It assumes the Old Testament's understanding of God, of care for the created world, of sexual love and of human creativity in art and music. It sees no need to repeat the deep insights of the Hebrew Scriptures into human suffering or the need for justice in society. On these and many other issues the Old Testament has more to say than the New.

◆ **As a matter of experience, people today continue to find that God speaks to them through the Old Testament writings.**

They are challenged and guided by its moral and social demands. They speak and listen to God through the Psalms. They see the patterns of God's work in their own lives as they read how he acted in Israel's history. Reading and hearing his book, they are drawn closer to him.

Reading and hearing the Old Testament, people are drawn closer to God.

9

Finding your way around

● ● ● ● ● ● ● ● ● ● ● ● ● ●

'**I** don't often visit our local library. To be honest, I'm embarrassed about not knowing where to find things.

'Everyone else seems to know exactly where to look for the romantic novels they want, or the books on sport or gardening. I know there are assistants there to help, but won't they think I'm silly for not understanding their ways of arranging things?'

Many people feel like that about the Old Testament.

It's too large, too full of ancient books with no clues about how to get started on them. And if you begin at the beginning it's OK for a while. But then you get stuck in complex rules about things like what to do with a dangerous bull and how to run a harvest festival.

Thankfully, every Bible has a contents page, so that if you're looking for the book of Joshua or Proverbs you can easily find out where it begins. And many modern

The books of the Old Testament

The Old Testament isn't just one book - it's thirty-nine of them. Some parts of the Christian Church - Roman Catholics, for example - include a number of other books in their Bibles. These are known as Deutero-canonical books.

THE LAW

Genesis, Exodus, Leviticus, Numbers, Deuteronomy

HISTORY AND STORY

Joshua, Judges, Ruth, 1 Samuel, 2 Samuel, 1 Kings, 2 Kings, 1 Chronicles, 2 Chronicles, Ezra, Nehemiah, Esther

POETRY AND WISDOM

Job, Psalms, Proverbs, Ecclesiastes, Song of Solomon

PROPHETS

Isaiah, Jeremiah, Lamentations, Ezekiel, Daniel, Hosea, Joel, Amos, Obadiah, Jonah, Micah, Nahum, Habakkuk, Zephaniah, Haggai, Zechariah, Malachi

Bibles have a short introduction to each biblical book to give you clues about how to approach it. You will find this, for example, in some editions of the *Good News Bible* and of the *New International Version*.

The Old Testament is actually a collection of thirty-nine books written over hundreds of years. The Jews divided it into three parts:

◆ **The Law (or 'Pentateuch') was the first five books.**

◆ **The Prophets included not only the books of prophets like Isaiah (which they called 'the latter prophets') but also the historical books from Joshua to 2 Chronicles ('the former prophets'). The reason for this was that the Jews saw 'history' not simply as a record of events but as the arena in which God acts and speaks. Both 'former' and 'latter' prophets were accounts of how God acted and spoke to his people Israel.**

◆ **The Writings were all the other books— including the poetry of Psalms and Job, short stories like Ruth and Esther, and the love poem called the Song of Songs.**

When the Hebrew Bible was translated into Greek for the benefit of Jews and others who were not very familiar with Hebrew, the order of the books was changed. There were now four sections—the Law, History and Story, Poetry and Wisdom books, and Prophets. This is the arrangement followed in most English Bibles.

In addition, more divisions were added later: into chapter and verse. This makes it easier to find a specific part of a particular book of the Old Testament. For instance, there are two books of Samuel. So the reference 1 Samuel 3:2 will mean the first book of Samuel, chapter 3, verse 2.

The first book of
| Samuel
| | chapter 3
| | | verse 2
| | | |
1 Samuel 3 : 2

> *I found consolation in the Bible. Not 'This is just a test' kind of consolation, but comfort from the real, immediate voices of people who had suffered greatly, and in ways that seemed close to what I was going through. I read the Bible more than fifty times in those first few years.*
>
> Terry Anderson, hostage in Lebanon
> (to journalists on his release)

When you read a modern book, it helps to know at the start what kind of a book it is. We have different expectations, and different ways of reading, a detective novel, a biography or a cookery book. When we read the Old Testament, it helps to know what kind of a book it is that we are reading. We will approach Psalms in a different way from Joshua, for example—one is poetry, the other is history.

There is a whole library here, reflecting the variety of people's experiences of God and responses to him. It can speak to our many different needs and situations. It's not always easy to get into, but it's worth the effort!

A created world

The book of Genesis begins with an account of the creation of the world: 'In the beginning God created the heavens and the earth' (Genesis 1:1). The God who wants to make himself known to men and women is responsible for the whole of creation.

The story in Genesis 1 isn't a scientific report about how the world began. Science has its own contribution to make to our understanding of the origins of the world. But the Bible has something to say through this story which science cannot say: not *how* the world was made, but *why*. The world didn't happen by chance, but is the product of a purposeful Creator.

Human beings tend to be most interested in their own place in God's creation. But most of Genesis 1 focuses on the rest of the created world—sun, moon, plants and animals, and so on. Humanity is the climax of God's creative plan, but not the be-all and end-all.

This is a vital message for today's world. The instruction that we should 'rule over' the rest of creation doesn't give us permission to exploit it. We abuse our responsibility if we turn forests into deserts, put animal species out of existence or pollute the atmosphere with the results of our extravagant use of natural resources.

For 'ruling' is the role of a king or queen. And in the Bible, monarchs are expected to use their power as God uses power—with care for those committed to their charge.

To be human involves sharing in God's care for the world—both the whole human race and the natural world—because we are entrusted with that responsibility by God himself.

3

The story of God and his people

● ● ● ● ● ● ● ● ● ● ● ● ● ●

The Old Testament is full of stories. But they are all part of one big story. It is the story of God inviting a particular group of people to get to know him, so that in the long run the whole world may learn to know and love him.

Before looking at the different parts of the Old Testament it will help us to have a sense of the overall story of what happened to those people. It goes something like this . . .

A long time ago there was a man called Abraham who lived in the land between the Euphrates and Tigris rivers, in modern Iraq. God told him to move with his family to Canaan, four hundred miles away. God promised to provide a homeland there for his descendants, and to make of them a special nation through whom the whole world would find blessing.

Abraham's family prospered in Canaan for three generations. But a famine caused them to seek refuge in Egypt. There after a while they became slaves, working on the building projects of the Egyptian kings, the pharaohs.

The Land

Today's debates over possession of the land of Israel echo a central theme of the Old Testament.

At the beginning of the history of the Jewish people, Abraham received from God the promise: 'To your offspring I will give this land' (Genesis 12:7). It was to be a place of security, a place which they could call home and where their special relationship with God could develop.

They conquered it under Joshua, defended it under the kings, and lost it to the Assyrians and Babylonians. On their return from exile in Babylon they lived in it, but always under the rule of a foreign power—except for the years 142–63BC.

It is striking that the land is constantly referred to in the Old Testament as 'the land of the Canaanites'. They never forgot that it had belonged to another race. And Old Testament writers speak of it as God's gift, not as Israel's right.

If God had given it to them, he could also withdraw his protection when they turned away from him. The exile wasn't merely a national tragedy, it was an act of divine judgment on Israel's failure to live by God's law.

God gave to the people of Israel 'the most beautiful of all lands' (Ezekiel 20:6). But an Israel which fails to show justice and compassion to the vulnerable 'will not remain in the Lord's land' (Hosea 9:3). God's gifts can never be taken for granted.

But God hadn't forgotten them. He told a man called Moses to lead the people—now called Israelites—in a dramatic escape out of Egypt. This 'exodus' involved the miraculous crossing of the 'Red Sea'. The water was held back while the Israelites crossed over, and then poured down on Egyptian soldiers to prevent their pursuit of the escaping slaves.

During forty years of wandering through the desert to get back to Canaan, God gave them the Law which became the basis of their life as a people. And they always looked back to the exodus as God's very special act of liberation. They knew him as the God who acts in history to deliver the oppressed.

Under Joshua, Moses' successor, they established themselves in Canaan, 'the Promised Land'. But they constantly felt the threat of attack by neighbouring nations.

They wanted a king to make them more secure, and God gave them Saul, then David and Solomon. David especially was a great king who made their land secure against its enemies. Later generations saw David's reign as a golden age, an ideal time which they longed for God to repeat. Solomon was important as the builder of the temple, the centre of Israelite worship in Jerusalem.

But the danger of kings is that they come to enjoy their power too much. Solomon's son Rehoboam was oppressive, and most of the nation rebelled against him. They formed the northern kingdom of Israel, whilst Rehoboam and his successors retained the southern area around Jerusalem, known as Judah.

The northern kingdom lasted for two hundred years as a separate state, until it fell to the aggressive Assyrians. Many of its people were taken into exile in other parts of Assyria's empire, never again to return to their own land.

Judah continued for a further 135 years before another empire brought the kingdom to its end. Nebuchadnezzar of Babylon ravaged the land, destroyed

The Israelites always looked back to the exodus—their escape from slavery in Egypt—as God's act of liberation.

The story of Abraham and his descendants

1 (AROUND 1900 BC) Abraham leaves the city of Ur in Mesopotamia and journeys to the land of Canaan. He spends some time in Egypt in order to avoid a famine, and then returns to Canaan. He lives a nomadic lifestyle, and as he travels throughout Canaan, God promises him that all the land he sees will one day belong to his descendants.

2 (BETWEEN 1650 AND 1270 BC) Abraham's grandson Jacob and his children settle in Egypt. As their numbers increase they are seen as a threat by the rulers of Egypt who force them into slave labour.

Moses confronts the Egyptian pharaoh and leads the Israelites out of Egypt and into the desert. At Mount Sinai God gives them his laws. He instructs them to invade Canaan, but those sent to spy out the land return with a discouraging report. They remain in the desert 40 years before attacking Jericho and beginning the conquest of the land.

3 (1230 BC) The Israelites settle the land promised to Abraham and become the nation of Israel. But political tensions divide the country (930 BC) into the northern kingdom of Israel, with its capital at Samaria, and southern Judah with its capital at Jerusalem.

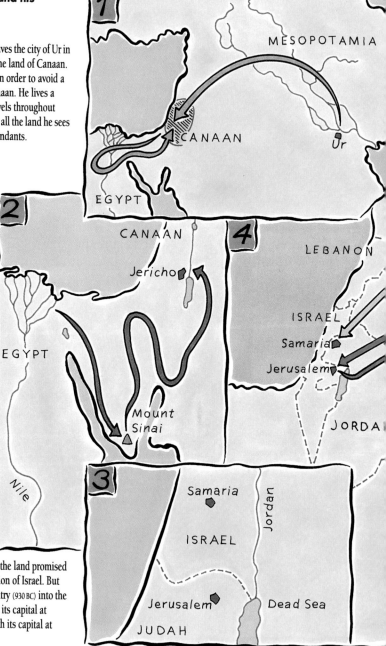

18

4 (722 – 538 BC) Israel generally rejects God, and the country is overrun by the Assyrians (green arrow), who take the people captive and scatter them throughout their huge empire.

The people of Judah vacillate between serving God and ignoring him. Judah survives Assyrian attacks, but later falls to Nebuchadnezzar, king of Babylon (blue arrow). The people of Judah are taken as prisoners to Babylon (red arrow). They remain there for 70 years until the Persians sack the city (brown arrow) and allow the Jews to return to Jerusalem.

The map indicates present-day boundaries: Persia is modern Iran.

Through much of history, the kingdoms of Israel and Judah were occupied by foreign powers—from the Assyrians and Babylonians to the Romans.

Jerusalem, and took all its leading citizens into exile in Babylon.

It was a devastating blow for a nation who believed that they enjoyed God's special protection. What price now their status as God's special people? Why had God let it happen?

Throughout the period of the kingdoms of Israel and Judah, God sent prophets, people who would communicate his will and explain his intentions to the people. Frequently they warned that the people's troubles were due to their ignoring God's will. They spoke of the consequences of disobedience, and the blessings which would come to an obedient people. But for most of the time the rulers and the people took no notice.

So disaster struck. But still God didn't forget them. In Babylon the Jews were able to maintain their religious and community life. And after fifty years Babylon itself fell victim to King Cyrus of Persia. He allowed Jewish people to return to their land and rebuild their lives.

Despite economic and social problems the temple was in due course rebuilt. Under Nehemiah the walls of Jerusalem were restored. Under Ezra the Law was written down and was listened to with new seriousness.

But still the Jews lived under Persian rule. They longed for freedom. Prophets spoke of a coming king who would set them free from all their enemies. But Persian rule gave way to rule by Alexander the Great of Greece, and then by Syrians.

The Syrian ruler Antiochus tried to force Jews to give up their faith. A loyal Jew named Judas, together with his brothers, led the 'Maccabean Revolt' against Antiochus. Their guerrilla tactics were successful, and for eighty years the Jews enjoyed independence from foreign control. Then came the Romans, who allowed the half-Jew Herod the Great to rule the land. Not until 1948 would there again be an independent Jewish state.

> *Christianity is inexplicable without Judaism. It simply is not possible to understand the world of the New Testament in isolation from its roots in the Near East and particularly against the background of Jewish culture, theology and life.*
>
> George Carey, Archbishop of Canterbury

The Jews believed that God acted in their history. They believed that God had given them the Law to show how they were meant to live as his people. But time and again they found themselves asking, 'How long, O Lord? How long till we are free from oppression? How long till we know in full the blessing you promised to Abraham?'

Yet through all that waiting they were discovering more of God, so that they could reveal God to the nations of the world. The Old Testament is their story. And it is God's story, recording how he made himself known during hundreds of years of history.

4

Laying the foundations

● ● ● ● ● ● ● ● ● ● ● ● ● ●

The first five books of the Bible belong together. The Jews called them 'the Law'. But they are much more than a collection of rules and regulations. The Hebrew word *Torah* means not just 'law' but 'guidance', 'instruction'. The Law laid the foundations of God's relationship with people.

These books offer guidance through stories as much as through lists of do's and don'ts. God makes himself known through events and experiences in people's lives.

The book of **Genesis** can be divided into two parts. The first part, chapters 1–11, sets Israel's story in the context of the world's story. So it begins with the world's creation. It then tells how human beings—Adam and Eve—challenge God's will for their lives. It shows how wrongdoing creeps into every aspect of human relationships and destroys our relationship with God.

But in Genesis 12–50 God makes a fresh start. His calling of Abraham and his descendants is his love in action. They are to be a 'pilot plant', a 'prototype', of the kind of life in relationship to him which he wants people

Abraham—receiver of promises

Abraham stands at the beginning of the story of God's people. To this day Jews speak of 'our father Abraham', and Christians too see him as a great example of trust in God.

His story, told in Genesis 11:27–25:11, cannot be checked historically with sources outside the Bible. Yet the social customs and the names which appear in this narrative fit with what archaeologists have discovered about conditions in the Middle East in the period 2000–1700BC.

Abraham was a city-dweller in the area which today is called Iraq. Prompted by God, he abandoned that lifestyle and set out with his family for the land of Canaan, 450 miles away. This journey was God's way of calling a person, a family, a nation to be the special bearers of his promise of blessing to the world.

When God called Abraham he promised to give him a land to live in, and descendants who would multiply to become a great nation. And he promised that through him all nations would find blessing.

Abraham's story tells of God's promise, obstacles which threatened that promise, and Abraham's faith which held on to the promise. As the story unfolds, God's promise comes under constant threat. How can Abraham and his family make their home in Canaan? It is already inhabited by Canaanites. His wife Sarah can't have children, so how can he have descendants? How can he make his home in the land when famine forces him to seek refuge in Egypt? But God's promises hold good, and so does Abraham's trust.

Even so, Abraham and Sarah are no too-good-to-be-true characters. While in Egypt Abraham saves his own skin by pretending that Sarah is his sister and making her marry the pharaoh. He goes along with her suggestion of having a child by her slave Hagar (which was a local custom). And Sarah laughs in disbelief that a woman past the menopause should have a baby.

Yet Abraham's faith shines through. He takes God at his word and does what he says. When called to leave the city for a nomadic life in Canaan, he goes. When he looks at the countless stars in the sky and senses God saying to him that his descendants will be as numerous as that, he believes him. He is always looking forward, trusting that the future is in God's hand, and sure enough, he and Sarah do have a son, Isaac.

But what can we make of that strange and troubling story in which God 'tested Abraham' by telling him to kill Isaac as a sacrifice? For Abraham the problem wasn't only that the idea seemed barbaric. To kill his son would be to destroy the one through whom God's promise of descendants was to be fulfilled.

The writer tells us that God's purpose was to test Abraham, to strengthen his faith. Abraham didn't know that. But though he must have been full of anguish at the danger to his son, he obeyed. His faith involved being willing to give up what was most dear to him. And he obeyed even when he couldn't see how God's plan would work out.

Sometimes people believe that God is calling them to act in a certain way, but can't see the purpose in it. Like Abraham, we can't see the end from the beginning. His story challenges us to risk everything for the sake of obedience to God. And it encourages us to trust that God's purpose will make sense in the long run.

Genesis 12–20

God calls Abraham
12:1–3

A child for Sarah
17:15–22, 21:1–7

The sacrifice of Isaac
22:1–19

Jacob tricks his brother
27:1–41

Joseph's story
37, 39–47

of all races eventually to experience.

Here then are stories full of drama and suspense. Will Abraham's wife Sarah have a baby, even though she is past the usual child-bearing age? Yes, because God will not fail to keep his promise to Abraham and Sarah that their descendents will become a great people.

There are stories about Abraham's son Isaac, and about Jacob, Isaac's scoundrel son. And then there is the story of Jacob's favourite son Joseph, a young man whose dreams fuelled big ideas about himself. He was sold as a slave by his jealous brothers and taken by traders to Egypt. There his skill at interpreting dreams eventually brought him to the pharaoh's attention and he was made Minister of Food Storage and Distribution—the second most powerful man in the kingdom.

Famine in Canaan forced Jacob's family to seek help in Egypt and brought them face to face with Joseph. In the end he and his brothers were reconciled and they all enjoyed the benefits of Joseph's wise planning.

The book of **Exodus** focuses on the role of Moses as Israel's liberator and lawgiver. After the famine Joseph's relations had settled in Egypt. But as they grew and prospered they became targets for the tyranny of later pharaohs. Moses, who had had a profound experience of God in the desert, was God's man for this moment.

The covenant or agreement between God and the people of Israel is at the heart of the book of Exodus

The heart of the book is in chapters 19–20. In chapter 20 God gives the people the Ten Commandments. But before that, in chapter 19, he reminds them of what he has already done by rescuing them from Egypt and speaks of the 'covenant' or 'agreement' which he is making with them.

In other words, God first acts to rescue people and bring them into relationship with himself. Then he gives them laws—guidance to keep the relationship healthy. In the Old Testament as in the New, God in his love makes the first move towards humanity, and calls us to respond in obedience.

Moses—liberator and lawgiver

As a Hebrew child brought up in an Egyptian palace, we might expect Moses to opt for a life of peace and luxury. But no. He became the leader of his enslaved people and challenged the tyranny of the Egyptian empire. God's message to the pharoah, 'Let my people go,' became his slogan. And in the end the pharaoh had no choice. He was helpless to stop Moses leading the Israelites from slavery to the Promised Land.

Such leadership didn't come easily to Moses. Like many of the Bible's great leaders, he was a reluctant hero. 'Who am I? How can I do it?' were his questions when he sensed God's call to lead the Israelites out of Egypt. 'I'll be with you,' said God. 'That's all the reassurance you need.'

So Moses argued with the pharaoh. He warned the pharaoh of the plagues which would afflict Egypt if he didn't show mercy to the Israelites. The pharaoh didn't change his mind, and the plagues came. Most of them were probably a series of natural phenomena following an unusually high flooding of the Nile—God using the workings of nature for his own purpose.

Finally, in the aftermath of the most terrible plague—the death of each first-born Egyptian son—the Israelites left Egypt. The pharaoh still tried to get his slave labour back by sending the army after them, only to have all the Egyptian soldiers and their chariots overwhelmed by the Red Sea which the Israelites had just crossed as though it were dry land.

The key event on the long journey to Canaan, the land promised to Abraham, whose descendents they were, took place at Mount Sinai. There God extended the 'covenant' agreement which he had already made with Abraham, by which he was committed to his people and they to him. In particular, he spelt out how they should respond to him by giving them the Ten Commandments.

There are many other laws in the books from Exodus to Deuteronomy, all of which Jews came to associate with Moses. They are, in a sense, an expansion of the basic commandments given at Sinai. Many of them remain today a challenge to the way we treat other people, such as: 'Do not ill-treat an alien or oppress him, for you were aliens in Egypt' and 'If you see the donkey of someone who hates you fallen down under its load, do not leave it there; be sure you help him with it'.

The people in the Bible are really alive. The things that bothered them, the temptations they were subject to, are just as relevant today.

I empathize with Moses because he came from two cultures; he was an Israelite brought up in Egypt. I come from two cultures: Jamaican and English. He was a very shy person and I'm very shy. I can understand how frightened he must have been of the things God asked him to do.

God still speaks through the Bible. It's a very lively book!

Josephine Campbell, publisher

The book of **Leviticus** consists of instructions about worship and festivals, and about what is involved in living as a 'holy people', a nation dedicated to God.

Numbers gets its name from the census of Israelites described in chapter one. Its Hebrew name, 'In the wilderness', describes its contents better. It tells of the Israelites' journey towards the Promised Land, how God provided for their needs and how they grumbled when things got tough. The journey of faith is a hard journey. But there are lessons to be learnt on the way, and God travels with us.

The book of **Deuteronomy** (meaning 'repetition of the law') presents Moses addressing the people on the edge of the Promised Land. He reminds them of what God has done for them, how he cares for them, and what kind of response he expects of them.

The God of Deuteronomy is the Lord of history who has brought Israel from Egypt to the Promised Land. He has made Israel his special people, his 'treasured possession'. Two words describing their response to him are particularly stressed in this book: they are to *remember* what he has done, and to *love* him. This remembering and love is expressed both in worship and in sensitive obedience to his will.

Moses sets before the people two choices for their national and community life:

See, I set before you today life and prosperity, death and destruction. For I command you today to love the Lord your God, to walk in his ways . . . then you will live and increase, and the Lord your God will bless you in the land you are entering to possess. But if your heart turns away and you are not obedient . . . you will not live long in the land you are crossing the Jordan to enter and possess.

DEUTERONOMY 30:15–18

In the book of Deuteronomy, Moses reminds the people of Israel how God has helped them in the past, and seeks their love for the future.

The Ten Commandments

The nature of these commandments is often misunderstood. People think of them as a negative list of 'Thou shalt nots'. But the Ten Commandments are rules to safeguard life, not to take the joy out of it.

God is providing boundaries within which people are to live. Within those boundaries there is freedom, not imprisonment, because these laws protect society from behaviour which would destroy it. If you send a group of children into a playground and tell them they can do anything they like, the result will not be freedom but chaos, and adults are not that different.

The Commandments begin with guidance about loyalty to the one God, who has freed his people from slavery. Then they move onto social relationships. The sabbath commandment protects the rights and health of workers.

Family life is safeguarded by the requirement to honour parents and to avoid adultery. The commandment not to kill asserts the value that God sets on every human being, and justice between people demands the prohibitions on theft, false accusation and the desire for others' goods which leads to conflict.

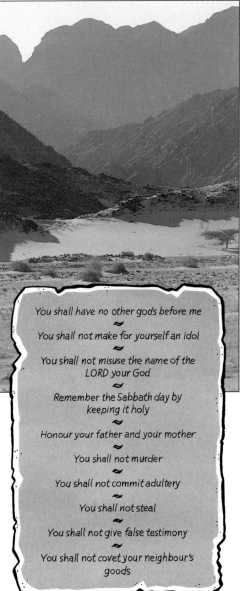

You shall have no other gods before me

You shall not make for yourself an idol

You shall not misuse the name of the LORD your God

Remember the Sabbath day by keeping it holy

Honour your father and your mother

You shall not murder

You shall not commit adultery

You shall not steal

You shall not give false testimony

You shall not covet your neighbour's goods

5

God in history

● ● ● ● ● ● ● ● ● ● ● ● ● ●

If someone invited us to tell our life story we could tell it in many different ways. For example, we could focus attention on our schooldays or our sporting achievements or our family life. We could explain why we made certain decisions which altered the course of our life.

But however we told the story, we would be choosing what we felt was important to us. And we would be telling the story from a particular point of view. My version of how I came to be punished at school for 'cheating' in an exam is not the same as my teacher's version.

In the same way, the story of a nation is told by choosing certain events as being especially significant. And it is told from a particular point of view, in order to make certain points. A British army general would not tell the story of British rule of India in the same way as an Indian cotton-picker.

Writing history involves giving shape to the story.

And you give shape to it by *choosing* what you see as important and explaining *why* you think it is important.

As we have seen, the Israelites who told the story of their escape from Egypt saw it as a great act of God. He had liberated them from slavery. That isn't how the Egyptian pharaoh's official historian would have told the story! Both the writer of Genesis and the Egyptian historian could agree that the event happened. But one of them saw in it the hand of God. The other would be working overtime to cover the cracks of a national economic and military disaster.

Hebrew historians wrote a connected record of the nation's history from their entry into the Promised Land under Joshua to the Babylonian exile six hundred years later. It is in the books of **Joshua**, **Judges**, **1 and 2 Samuel** and **1 and 2 Kings**. In it they explain events from a particular viewpoint.

They see history as the arena of God's activity. And they show how the nation's fortunes rose and fell according to whether the people and their rulers took

How you write history depends on your point of view. The Israelites saw history as the arena of God's activity.

Be strong and courageous. Do not be terrified; do not be discouraged, for the Lord your God will be with you wherever you go.

JOSHUA 1:9

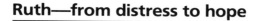

Ruth—from distress to hope

Tucked in between Judges and 1 Samuel, with their tales of war and politics, is the personal story of one woman, Ruth. The Israelites and the people of Moab to the east of the Jordan river were traditional enemies. But a family from Bethlehem settled in Moab during a famine. One of the men married Ruth, a Moabite woman.

After the tragic death of her husband and her father-in-law, Ruth goes with her widowed mother-in-law, Naomi, to Bethlehem, Naomi's home town. There, with Naomi's encouragement, she wins the love of another man from Naomi's family, Boaz. He marries her and brings joy to Naomi as the couple present her with a grandchild.

The story is beautifully told. But *why* is it told? In contrast to the larger-than-life characters and the national significance of the historical books, this story seems so small-scale, the people so ordinary. Perhaps that is the point, or at least part of it.

It is a story of God's involvement in the tragedies and joys of ordinary people. It shows how, at a time when violence and abuse of power hit the national headlines, there are still people living out a vivid faith in God.

Naomi, struck by the death of her husband and sons, picks up the pieces of her life and returns home. Gradually she overcomes her bitterness as she realizes that God has not abandoned her. And finally her joy is complete as she holds her grandson in her arms.

Ruth, a Moabite woman, discovers Israel's God and refuses all Naomi's pleas to do the 'sensible' thing and remain in her own country. 'Where you go I will go, and where you stay I will stay. Your people will be my people and your God my God' (Ruth 1:16). Human love can overcome the hostility of racism and nationalism.

Boaz, too, shows compassion, and acts responsibly towards his relatives and to the poor. He is an honourable man in the time of the judges—an age strewn with dishonourable men. But the dominant characters of this story are women, discovering God's care in the circumstances of ordinary life.

Two other themes are there for the reader to ponder. The fact that Ruth is not an Israelite is clearly important. The God of Israel accepts and shows faithfulness to all who come to him, whatever their background, and sometimes the people of Israel needed to be reminded of this.

And the final paragraph of the book reports that the child of Ruth and Boaz was the grandfather of King David. Israel's greatest king—and the Messiah descended from him—had a foreign woman among their ancestors!

God's law seriously. In other words, they show how God's promise and warning of Deuteronomy 30:15–18 that we looked at earlier came true in the experience of God's people.

The book of **Joshua** tells how the Israelites began to

establish themselves in Canaan. God's words to Joshua before the conquest begins are an encouragement to anyone taking on a demanding task in God's name:

Be strong and courageous. Do not be terrified; do not be discouraged, for the Lord your God will be with you wherever you go.

JOSHUA 1:9

The book of **Judges** shows how often they compromised their loyalty to God and were attacked by surrounding nations. And it records that when the people renewed their commitment to God he raised up leaders—'judges'—such as Deborah, Gideon and Samson to deliver them from their enemies.

Samuel, whose name is attached to two of these books, was a wise man of God and leader of Israel who bridged the gap between the judges and the kings. But in fact most of **1 and 2 Samuel**—the first and second books of Samuel—tell the story of the first two kings, Saul and David.

Worried about the strength of their Philistine enemies the people urged Samuel to appoint for them a king 'such as all the other nations have'. Samuel saw this as a failure of faith, a failure to trust God as their king. To want to be 'like other nations' was to deny their special calling to live by values different from those of other nations.

But God has a way of weaving even people's wrong choices into the pattern of his purpose. So he gave Israel a king—Saul. And then David, Solomon and the others who followed. The people learnt through hard experience that kings can bring not only benefits but hardships—forced labour, military conscription and taxes.

But they also learnt that God had a very special plan for David's family. One of his descendants would be the 'Messiah', God's chosen leader who would bring a new

Joshua
The fall of Jericho
5:13–6:27

Judges
Deborah
4:4–16
Gideon
6:1–8:28
Samson
13:1–16:31

1 Samuel
The people want a king
8:1–22
David and Goliath
17:12–51

2 Samuel
David and Bathsheba
11:1–12:25

David—flawed genius

David was a shepherd boy in Bethlehem when he was catapulted into the centre of his nation's history. Saul, the first king, was already proving a liability. Prompted by God, the old prophet Samuel anointed young David with oil—a sign that he was God's choice as the next king.

He soon came to Saul's attention when he killed Goliath the Philistine with a single stone from his sling. He was content to bide his time until Saul's death should open the way for David to replace him. But the popularity he gained by his feat against Goliath made Saul fiercely jealous of David. His paranoia made him try to kill David, who was forced to flee and become an outlaw.

Saul came with troops to hunt David down in his hiding place near the Dead Sea. Entering a cave to relieve himself, he had no idea that David and his friends were hiding at the back of the cave. David's friends urged him to kill Saul there and then. But he crept over and merely cut off a corner of his robe. 'I will not lift my hand against my master', he said, 'because he is the Lord's anointed'.

Saul committed suicide after losing a battle against the Philistines, and David became king first over his own tribe of Judah and then over the whole nation of Israel. He captured Jerusalem, which until then had always remained in Canaanite hands, and made it his capital city. This building of a capital in a neutral place was a shrewd move, calculated to minimize jealousy between the various tribal groups of Israel.

David squashed the power of the Philistines once and for all. He extended Israel's territory in other directions and made his country strong. He made Jerusalem the centre of Israel's worship, and received from God the promise that his son would build a temple there. Through the prophet Nathan God promised to show his love to David's descendants for ever. 'Your house and your kingdom shall endure for ever before me; your throne shall be established for ever.'

David was grateful to God for giving him success in all he did. But his next encounter with the prophet Nathan was not to be so comfortable.

One evening he looked down from the roof of his hill-top palace and saw a beautiful woman called Bathsheba bathing. A king gets used to getting what he wants, and David wanted Bathsheba. His obsession with her led him to arrange the death of her husband and to marry her.

Then Nathan came and told him a story about a rich man who stole a lamb from a poor man. David's sense of justice made him side with the poor man: 'As surely as the Lord lives, the man who did this deserves to die!'

'You're the man!', replied Nathan.

The story makes no excuses for David. He did wrong and he suffered for it. Yet he had the courage to admit his wrong and make a fresh start. So despite his mistakes he was remembered as a great king. In the books of Kings no verdict on a ruler is so positive as the words, 'He walked in all the ways of his father [ancestor] David.'

And when the Jews longed for a future king to put an end to all their troubles, it was a king 'like David' that they looked for.

kind of freedom and peace to humanity.

So Israel's desire for a king was from one viewpoint a failure of faith. Yet God made it the means through which he would show his love to humanity in a fuller way. Israel's God isn't distant and unchanging. God has given us free will to choose whether or not to obey him, but he isn't defeated by human disobedience. He adjusts to it and through it finds another way to make known his loving plan for the world.

1 and 2 Kings continue the story from Solomon's reign and his building of the temple right through to Nebuchadnezzar's destruction of Jerusalem and the exile which followed.

God rarely intervenes in dramatic or miraculous ways in these narratives. He is more like the manager of a football team than a player on the field. But all the time he is there, involved with events. All the time the nation is experiencing the truth of those words from Deuteronomy—life and blessing follow obedience to God's way, but disaster follows when people turn away from his will and his protection.

Most of 1 and 2 Kings is the story of constant compromise between trust in the living God and the old nature gods of Canaan. It is the story of a nation which has lost its vision of what it means to be God's people, showing other nations how God wants them to be.

Even the two rulers who were genuinely faithful to God—Hezekiah and Josiah—could not delay for long the judgment which was to come through the downfall of Judah and the exile to Babylon. That event in 587BC shook the faith of God's people to its foundations. But even in that disaster hope was reborn.

1 and 2 Chronicles retell the story of the books of Samuel and Kings for people of a later period. They draw out new lessons from history for Israelites returning from the Babylonian exile and trying to rebuild their lives, especially about the importance of worship.

1 Kings

The wisdom of Solomon
3:1–28

Elijah and the prophets
of Baal
18:1—19:18

2 Kings

Elisha cures Naaman of
leprosy
5:1–14

The siege of Jerusalem
18:13—19:36

The books of **Ezra** and **Nehemiah** continue the story from this perspective into the period after the Jews had returned from Babylon. They tell of the return to Palestine, the rebuilding of the temple, Nehemiah's rebuilding of the walls of Jerusalem and Ezra's bringing of the law back to the centre of the nation's life.

These two books grapple with the question how God's people are to relate to the world around them which does not share their faith. They show how the Persian authorities were quite sympathetic to Ezra and Nehemiah. God can use foreign powers to provide stability for his people.

2000BC	▼1800BC	▼1600BC	▼1400BC	▼1200BC
	Abraham arrives in Canaan	Abraham's descendants arrive in Egypt	Exodus from Egypt	Israelites arrive in Canaan
			Moses ⬆	Dav
⬆ Abraham				
		Abraham's descendants living in Egypt (now known as Israelites)		Ruth ⬆
				Samuel ⬆
E G Y P T		The story of the Jewish people (shown by the green horizontal band) set against a background of contemporary empires.		A S S Y R I A

The story of the Jewish people (shown by the green horizontal band) set against a background of contemporary empires.

On the other hand, the concern of the Jewish leaders to avoid the watering down of their people's unique faith led them to ban mixed marriages with non-Jews. This harsh teaching seemed necessary to them if Judaism was to maintain its distinctive mission to the world.

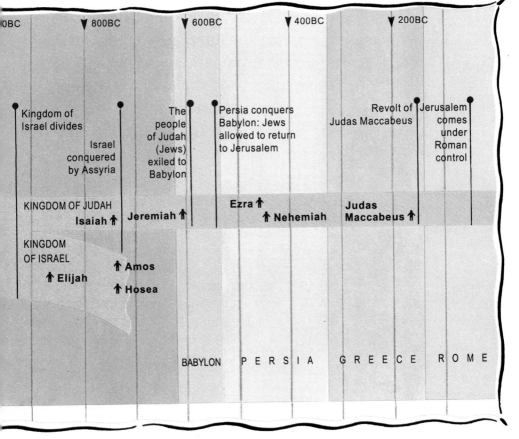

6

Speaking for God

● ● ● ● ● ● ● ● ● ● ● ● ● ●

Sometimes today we speak of someone as a 'prophet'. We may mean that they have a gift for seeing how the future will unfold. Or that they have something to say which challenges the assumptions and values of our society. We may take little notice of them. Yet deep down we suspect that there is truth in what they say. There were prophets in Israel like that.

God had high hopes for his people. He longed for them to walk wholeheartedly in the way that was best for them. But constantly they got side-tracked. Many were attracted to the nature worship of neighbouring peoples, which made no moral demands on them and positively encouraged sexual laxity. Many, especially the more wealthy, lived for themselves rather than for their community, following the rituals of worship but being unjust to the poor. They lost sight of their calling to be an example to other nations of how God wanted people to live.

The prophets were God's agents through whom he appealed to them to get back on the right track. They spoke words of criticism and encouragement, of hope and warning. They were mostly 'outsiders' who had no official position in the state or in the religious establishment. But they had an intense vision of the sickness at the heart of society. And they suffered for their outspokenness.

Small groups of followers preserved their words in writing, and these now form the last part of the Old Testament. The order in which the prophetic books appear bears no relation to the order in which they lived. Three of the earliest ones were Amos, Hosea and Isaiah.

God and politics

The Old Testament story took place against a background of ambition and power, war and politics.

Worried about the strength of the nations around them, the people of Israel urged Samuel to appoint for them a king 'such as all the other nations have' (1 Samuel 8:5). First Saul and then David became kings of Israel, and it became a military power to be reckoned with.

King Solomon, David's son, was famous for his foreign alliances, his building schemes and his extravagant lifestyle. Forced labour was the price the people paid for his achievements.

When he died the question bubbled to the surface: would his son Rehoboam continue Solomon's oppression, or would he learn a different way to rule? The story is told in 1 Kings 11:41—12:20.

When representatives of the Israelite tribes met to affirm Rehoboam's kingship, one of them, whose name was Jeroboam, said: 'Your father put a heavy yoke on us, but now lighten the harsh labour and the heavy yoke he put on us and we will serve you.'

Rehoboam consulted two sets of advisers. His older advisers knew that there was another way of exercising power: 'If today you will be a servant to these people, they will always be your servants.' But his brash young contemporaries urged even greater oppression.

They won the day, and the fortunes of the nation were changed for ever. Rehoboam increased his tyranny and Jeroboam led a successful rebellion against him. Aiming at despotic control, Rehoboam lost most of his subjects.

From then on there were two kingdoms—Israel in the north, ruled by Jeroboam and his successors, and Judah in the south, ruled by Rehoboam and his descendants. Conflict between them rumbled on till there was little left to fight about, and they in turn fell victim to the superpowers of Assyria and Babylon.

Political power can be used to oppress people and promote injustice. Or it can be used to serve people and to build a just and tolerant community. The Old Testament political commentators were clear about which approach God favoured; the fall of both Israel and Judah was unmistakeably linked to their injustice.

Amos speaks to those who are comfortable while others suffer injustice.

Amos lived around 750BC, when the northern kingdom of Israel was separated from the southern kingdom, Judah. A shepherd from Judah, he went to prophesy in Israel. No wonder the people of the north called him an interfering busybody when he started denouncing their religious and economic life!

He warned them that God was unimpressed by all their religious worship whilst their daily lives were full of injustice. He warned them that the future which they saw so filled with hope was in fact laden with doom for them. And so it was. In 722BC the Assyrians conquered Israel and took the leading citizens into exile.

The message of Amos undermines the comfortable assumption that we have a right to an ever-increasing standard of living, whether or not we act with justice and compassion towards others.

Hosea's message of God's love for his disobedient people was echoed in his own reconciliation with his unfaithful wife.

Hosea spoke in Israel at about the same time. He focused on the problem which underlay the corruption of the nation's life—its turning away from God. Having himself married an unfaithful wife, he had special insight into how God felt about Israel's 'adultery'. From his own experience of being guided by God to seek out his wife and remake the marriage, he spoke of God's forgiving love for Israel.

Hosea's deep insight into God's care for humanity didn't lead him to be sentimental about it or to take it for granted. Knowing the lengths to which God's love would go, he warned all the more urgently of the pain which follows rejection of it.

Isaiah showed the kings of his day how closely God and politics were linked.

Isaiah lived a generation later in Jerusalem, capital of the southern kingdom. At that time the threat which Assyria posed to the northern kingdom spelt danger for Judah also. One day in the temple he had a breathtaking vision of God's greatness and holiness, which shaped his view of the nation and its prospects.

He denounced in Judah similar sins to those found by Amos in Israel. All such injustice and inhumanity was a

[The word of the Lord] is in my heart like a burning fire, shut up in my bones. I am weary of holding it in; indeed, I cannot.

JEREMIAH 20: 9

Jeremiah—prophet of crisis

Jeremiah was a prophet for forty turbulent years (from 626BC until after the destruction of Jerusalem in 587). The mighty empires of Assyria and Egypt were on the wane, and Babylon was rising fast. Three episodes in Jeremiah's life will give a picture of his career.

Scene 1: about 609BC Assyria's empire had been swallowed up by that of Babylon, and Judah's relations with Egypt were not friendly. But the people who ought to be worried were not over-concerned. Surely the God who had delivered Jerusalem from Sennacherib in 701BC would do the same again? After all, he would not allow his temple to come to harm.

Jeremiah addressed people at the temple gate as they came to worship: 'Do not trust in deceptive words and say, "The temple of the Lord, the temple of the Lord, the temple of the Lord!"' The genuine trust in God of a century before had now become just a slogan. The very people who came flooding to the temple kept their real enthusiasm for the Canaanite nature gods. And the nation was morally bankrupt.

Jeremiah's career as a prophet and as a human being nearly ended there and then. But thanks to a friend he was saved from attack by the crowd (Jeremiah 7 and 26).

Scene 2: 604BC It was a day of fasting, ordered because of the national crisis. Babylonian armies threatened the land, and all Jeremiah's earlier warnings of invasion now seemed plausible after all. Jeremiah asked his secretary Baruch to write on a scroll all his previous prophecies and read them to the people at the temple.

King Jehoiakim, sitting by the fire in his winter palace, got wind of what had happened. The scroll was brought and read to him. After three or four columns had been read, the king grabbed the scroll, cut off the part that had been read and threw it on the fire. Section by section the whole scroll was read, cut and burnt to cinders.

When Jeremiah got news of this, he asked Baruch to write it all out again. The prophet's words must be preserved, so that in due course people could judge for themselves whether he had truly understood the mind of God.

Scene 3: 587BC Babylonian armies surrounded Jerusalem. Jeremiah was under house arrest, to stop his gloomy messages depressing the people any further. His cousin Hanamel arrived wondering if Jeremiah would like to buy a field at Anathoth.

This was Jeremiah's home village, a few miles north of Jerusalem. To own a field there was a nice idea. There was only one problem. The whole area was swarming with Babylonian soldiers. Yet Jeremiah solemnly weighed out seventeen shekels of silver and had the correct legal documents drawn up.

Now people had a different reason for thinking that Jeremiah was crazy. Why should a prophet of doom buy land occupied by the enemy who was about to bring utter ruin to Jerusalem and force its people into exile?

But it was an act of hope by a man convinced that beyond judgment lay a new beginning. The exile would last for a generation, but what then? 'This is what the Lord Almighty, the God of Israel, says: Houses, fields and vineyards will again be bought in this land' (Jeremiah 32).

In this act of hope, as in his earlier warnings of destruction, Jeremiah turned out be be right. If the value of a prophet is measured by his success in persuading his audience, Jeremiah was a failure. But if being a prophet is about listening to God and telling others what God has said, whatever the personal consequences, then he was one of the greatest.

denial of the relationship the people claimed with the holy God. He warned Ahaz the king that his desperate attempts to make alliances with one foreign nation against others would recoil on his head. His message was, 'Trust God, even when times are dark. You are safer with him than with any amount of playing at power politics.'

Isaiah found a more responsive king in Ahaz's son and successor Hezekiah. When the Assyrian emperor Sennacherib invaded Judah in 701BC God promised him through Isaiah, 'He will not enter this city or shoot an arrow here . . . I will defend this city and save it, for my sake and for the sake of David my servant'. And so it proved. Most of Sennacherib's huge army was destroyed by a plague and he withdrew without delay.

Other parts of Isaiah's prophecy warned that God would punish the people of Judah with exile if they didn't abandon their ungodly ways. But beyond exile there was a new beginning for a nation trusting God which would bring blessing to the nations around it.

Chapters 40–55 probably don't come from Isaiah himself but from a later prophet while the people of Judah were in exile in Babylon. His message responds with hope to the agonized questions they must have asked:

Had God been defeated by the gods of Babylon?

No, replied the prophet, he was the creator of all things, more powerful than any other force in the universe.

Had he let Judah down by allowing them to suffer like this?

No, they had let him down, and their exile was the consequence of their unfaithfulness.

Had he abandoned them for ever?

No—he was about to restore them to Judah.

The prophets continually called God's people back to holiness and justice.

God's miracles of deliverance aren't confined to the past. If he enabled the Israelites to escape from Egypt he will arrange a new 'exodus' to bring them again to the Promised Land. There they will rediscover their role as his servant and renew their mission to bring light to the world.

Isaiah 55–66 reflects the time when many of the exiles had already returned to Judah. Faced with the enormous task of rebuilding their society, they needed all the encouragement which this prophet could give. He offered a vision not only of a new Jerusalem but of a universe transformed.

But such a glorious future doesn't come without the cooperation of God's people. The holy God requires a holy people. As bluntly and as passionately as Amos, this prophet described the kind of life in society which God demands.

The Messiah

The Jews believed that God had begun to free his people through his action in the lives of Abraham and Moses. He was committed to them and was going to carry his plan through to the end.

But they knew that life was often painful and unfair—not at all as it should be if God was totally in charge of things. They knew too that the kings who were meant to rule them well were often unjust and unfaithful to God. There was little sign that a world of perfect justice and peace would come through them. So how were things going to change?

Prophets brought the vision of an ideal future king, a descendant of the great King David who would be called 'Wonderful Counsellor, Mighty God, Everlasting Father, Prince of Peace'. When he came he would 'proclaim peace to the nations'. The earth would be 'full of the knowledge of the Lord as the waters cover the sea' (Isaiah 9:2–7; 11:1–9; Micah 5:2; Zechariah 9:9–13).

Later this expected bringer of peace and freedom was called 'the Messiah'. This is simply a Hebrew word meaning 'the anointed one'. Kings were anointed—they had oil smeared or poured on their heads—as a sign that they were appointed by God to their role of leadership among God's people.

The deliverer for whom the Jews longed was to be a kingly figure, descended from David. He would be God's way of bringing to the world God's triumph over evil, suffering and death.

Was all this just wishful thinking? Were they inventing a hope of better times to come merely to help them cope with their present distress?

We might draw that conclusion, except for two things. First, their hope for the future was not simply invented out of nothing. It was based on their past experience of God, which gave them confidence that he wouldn't leave his work unfinished.

Secondly, Christians believe that Jesus, 'great David's greater son', is the Messiah who was promised. We no longer have to hope for someone to turn up. Through Jesus God has already responded to the longings of his people. The Old Testament story is an unfinished story. But beyond it lies its completion in the story of Jesus told in the New Testament.

The thing that hit me between the eyes were the Messianic prophecies from the part of the Scriptures Christians call the Old Testament, our territory, the Tanach. I was familiar with the hit stories—Moses, David, Solomon, Esther—but I'd never read or heard these bits before. Or that Messiah had been prophesied. I'd seen various quotes on Christmas cards. Things like 'For to us a child is born, to us a son is given; and the government will be upon his shoulder, and his name will be called "Wonderful counsellor, Mighty God, Everlasting Father, Prince of Peace," '. But I'd always thought they came from the New Testament. Now I realized that was in Isaiah 9:6. One of ours!

Helen Shapiro, singer

7

Poetry and wisdom

• • • • • • • • • • • • •

There are times when we feel like singing for joy or shouting in anger at things that happen to us. There are times when we are in deep despair. There are times when we are full of doubt, when we long to ask God why things are as they are.

The Old Testament has space for all these emotions. The fact that they are included there suggests that God gives us permission to express them. He doesn't want people to pretend that they are feeling great and are full of faith when they are not. He expects people to be honest with him—and with each other.

Proverbs, Job and Ecclesiastes are called 'wisdom books', because they express the thoughts of the wise about how life works. Unlike other books we have looked at, their ideas aren't closely tied in with the life and history of Israel. They deal with questions about what it means to be human. And they sometimes draw on the teachings of the wise in other countries such as Babylon and Egypt. A true insight is a true insight, wherever it comes from.

Proverbs deals with everyday experiences of life. It is a collection of short sayings which often make us smile. They invite us to reflect on our own attitudes and actions and to ask: Is this wisdom or folly? For instance:

Like a gold ring in a pig's snout is a beautiful woman who shows no discretion.

PROVERBS 11:22

The lazy man says, 'There is a lion outside. I shall be killed if I go out on the street!'

PROVERBS 22:13

If a man loudly blesses his neighbour early in the morning, it will be taken as a curse.

PROVERBS 27:14

The book of Proverbs shows God's wisdom at work in everyday life.

The value of all this is that it makes religious people keep their feet on the ground. Those people who are so spiritual that they lack common sense need a daily dose of Proverbs.

If Proverbs was the only wisdom book, we might conclude that Israel's wise men were a rather optimistic bunch of people who hadn't faced up to the dark side of life. But the book of Job breathes a very different atmosphere. One of the finest poems in the whole of world literature, it asks why innocent people suffer.

Job is a good man overwhelmed by the most extreme suffering. Three friends come to 'comfort' him. 'Your suffering must be due to sins which you have secretly committed. You can't be as good as we all thought. So ask God's forgiveness, and maybe he will restore you.'

Job takes a straight look at the problem of undeserved suffering.

This is as helpful to Job as a tin-opener to a drowning man. In the end God himself speaks. Yet he doesn't give a straight answer to Job's question, 'Why am I suffering?' He says, in effect, 'Will you trust me to run the world according to my wisdom?'

45

The Psalms—many responses to the one God

What kind of God did the people of the Old Testament believe in? Because the Psalms express Israel's response to God in varied circumstances, they show us what God meant to them.

God is Creator of the whole world. He delights in it and wants humanity to enjoy it and care for it.

How many are your works, O Lord!
In wisdom you made them all;
the earth is full of your creatures.
Psalm 104:24

God acts in history, especially in the experience of his people Israel.

He saved them for his name's sake,
to make his mighty power known.
He rebuked the Red Sea, and it dried up;
he led them through the depths as through a desert.
Psalm 106:8–9

God desires to show mercy and forgiveness.

The Lord is compassionate and gracious,
slow to anger, abounding in love...
He does not treat us as our sins deserve
or repay us according to our iniquities.
Psalm 103:8, 10

But he opposes those who resist his purpose, especially those who oppress the powerless and deny justice to the poor. He holds people to account for their lives.

Rise up, O Judge of the earth;
pay back to the proud what they deserve.
How long will the wicked, O Lord,
how long will the wicked be jubilant?
Psalm 94:2–3

God guides his people through the Bible.

Your word is a lamp to my feet
and a light for my path.
Psalm 119:105

God draws close to those who bring to him their needs and anxieties.

The Lord is my shepherd, I shall not be in want..
Even though I walk through the valley of the
shadow of death,
I will fear no evil, for you are with me;
your rod and your staff, they comfort me.
Psalm 23:1, 4

Though God seems sometimes not to protect his people and their faith is severely strained, he remains their source of hope. They would rather live with the question why he seems to be hidden from them than abandon trust in him.

How long will the enemy mock you, O God?
Will the foe revile your name for ever?
Why do you hold back your hand, your right
hand?...
But you, O God, are my king from of old;
You bring salvation upon the earth.
Psalm 74:10–11

God will one day set all things right and establish his rule over all the world.

He comes to judge the earth.
He will judge the world in righteousness
and the peoples in his truth.
Psalm 96:13

There is no tidy answer to why suffering affects the innocent. But beyond the anger and the questions we may discover God's presence. He isn't remote, blaming us for our wrongdoing. He is waiting to be discovered as the friend who stands beside us in our suffering.

Ecclesiastes ('the philosopher') perhaps rings more bells in our day than any other book of the Bible. Its author seems to hover between faith and doubt, between enjoyment of life and puzzlement about life's meaning.

'Utterly meaningless!', he says, 'Everything is meaningless!'. He has tried all the normal routes to find satisfaction and meaning to life—pleasure, money, philosophy, hard work, power over others. But there is always a craving for more. And sooner or later death puts a full stop to everyone's life. What meaning is left then? Yet at the same time he feels that life is a gift of God, and that to obey God's commandments is 'the whole duty of mankind'.

Like many people today this writer stumbles between these two reactions. He feels that the meaning of life is always out of his reach, and that death mocks so much of human achievement, and yet that it is right to enjoy the good things of life.

Perhaps there is no real answer to his questions, unless death itself can be conquered. But that is a question to which the New Testament offers a fuller answer than can be found within the Old Testament.

The Psalms are the hymn-book and prayer-book of

The book of Ecclesiastes echoes the modern dilemma of trying to find meaning in a contradictory world.

The Psalms offer us words for every human situation and emotion.

> *I found great solace in reading the Psalms. The anguished suffering mind that had created them and had cried out to God in his suffering reflected much of our own condition. Exhausted with profound questions and never finding an answer, we took relief in devotional moments.*
>
> Brian Keenan, held hostage in Lebanon for four and a half years

the Jews. In biblical times the sound of their words filled the temple in Jerusalem, and they continue to be sung by Jews and Christians today. They show us a lot about how the Israelites expressed their faith and hope, their thanks and fears to God. Different kinds of psalms provide words for different needs and occasions.

There is variety here to speak to every human emotion and situation. The book of Psalms can suggest to us what to say to God when we have no words for what we are feeling.

They show us that it is all right to question God, to throw at him our anger and our frustration. They show how we can take encouragement in a present crisis by recalling how God has dealt with past crises. They remind us too that even when we feel most alone we can be part of a community of faith.

Even when we feel most alone, we can be part of a community of faith.

The Old Testament on trial

• • • • • • • • • • • • •

A book which aims to introduce people to the Old Testament shouldn't hide the difficulties which are there. Here are three issues which often puzzle people.

How does God speak?

Stories in the Bible often include phrases such as 'God said to Abraham'. This presents a problem to modern readers.

Should we conclude that God had a special way of getting his message over to people in those days, which he doesn't use today? Or that the biblical writers were simply imagining that God spoke to people?

Today God might speak through a friend's advice or through a certain situation. Sometimes there may be a growing conviction over a period of time that we should make some major change in our lives.

At other times, words from the Bible can make a strong impression. They seem to come as a special message from God about our own situation. And I have met people who believed so strongly that God was speaking to them about something that it really felt as though they could *hear* his voice.

God spoke to people in Old Testament times as he speaks to us today.

God spoke to people in Old Testament times in similar ways. The writers' vivid way of story-telling led them to write simply, 'God said to Abraham . . .'. But those simple words probably reflect the variety of experiences which believers in God have today.

The God whom Christians worship today is the same God who called Abraham. And he wants to tell us, too, how to live.

But when we try to listen to what God is saying we are often not sure whether it is really him speaking. Maybe I feel he is calling me to speak in public. But is that really his will for me, or is it just because I enjoy talking?

It takes time and experience to be sure that God is really speaking in a particular way. The Old Testament writers had both. Those who wrote the story of Abraham were collecting memories passed on through generations of storytellers.

By the time they wrote they couldn't know exactly how God's extraordinary call had come to Abraham, and how he was persuaded to leave security behind and set off for Canaan.

But they knew he had made that journey. And they could see with hindsight that it really had been a journey planned and guided by God. They could see that it was the start of a continuing story in which God was guiding his people and showing them his loving purpose for the world.

Why is the Old Testament so full of blood and guts?

Our world is weary of war and the monstrous treatment of men and women which goes with it. So it isn't surprising that we find it distasteful to read so often of

The Old Testament world is not so different from our own—nations still struggle for power, killing the innocent in the process.

wars and violence, particularly in the historical books of the Old Testament.

But perhaps that is the place to begin thinking about the problem. The fighting is there because the Old Testament world wasn't so different from our own. Then, as now, nations wrestled for power over each other, abusing their fellow human beings in the process.

And it was inevitable that the Israelites would be caught up in this because their land was vulnerable to invasion from all directions. From ancient times until the present day the armies of Egypt, Assyria, Babylon, Greece, Rome, the Arabs and the Turks have seen control of this land as the key to control of the Middle East.

The real problem is not that war figures so much in the stories, but that the Israelites *used* war to establish themselves in Canaan under Joshua's leadership. And that—according to the Old Testament—God *told* them to kill all the inhabitants of the Canaanite cities which they conquered. What can be said about that?

◆ **When they came to Canaan the Israelites themselves were landless refugees.**

Only people who have been in that situation can really understand what it's like to lack the security of home and land.

◆ **The reason given for such drastic treatment of conquered Canaanites was that if they survived they might lead the Israelites to abandon the true God and engage in the perverted worship of Canaanite gods.**

At a critical period of their history, maybe the Israelites were simply not strong enough in their faith to be able to cope with the Canaanites and their religion.

◆ **The Old Testament writers also took for granted that God uses the events of war to pass judgment on wicked people.**

The same book of Deuteronomy warns that the Israelites themselves would be the victims of defeat in war if they turned away from God and his protection—a prophecy which was ultimately fulfilled. In the long run it is right, not might, which prevails in the affairs of nations.

◆ **The Old Testament lays down limits on what is permitted in war.**

These constraints contrasted sharply with the 'anything goes' approach of some neighbouring countries. For instance, if laying siege to a city the Israelites could cut down trees to build siege works, but could not take fruit-bearing trees. Out of respect for life, this law forbade the kind of ruthless destruction which the Assyrians later made famous and which has become such a horrifying part of modern warfare.

◆ **Out of Israel's later experience of defeat in war came the realization that God's way for his people was not one of military victory.**

In Isaiah 40–55 (especially chapter 53) Israel is pictured as God's servant. This servant is to be gentle and, when necessary, to accept suffering. God's purpose for the world comes about not when his people try to solve their problems through force, but when they realize that out of suffering he can bring life for the world.

The description of the 'suffering servant' in the book of Isaiah foreshadows God's plan of bringing life for the world out of suffering.

Isn't it all fairy stories?

For many people the Old Testament is a collection of stories on the same level as Father Christmas or the tooth fairy.

But different parts of the Old Testament are different types of literature. They need approaching in different ways.

Some books, such as Proverbs or Psalms, make no claim to be historical. The story of Jonah and the 'whale'

Discovered in 1880, Hezekiah's water tunnel was originally built to ensure a fresh water supply to Jerusalem in case of siege.

Also discovered over 100 years ago, is this cylinder which dates from 536BC. It records how Cyrus took Babylon and freed people to return to their original homes.

Archaeological discoveries such as these help to authenticate events from this part of the Bible.

was probably never intended as an account of historical events. It is a story which through humour and irony makes its point about God's love even for Israel's enemies.

The very beginning of Genesis takes us back to the beginnings of time, illustrating the nature of human experience and revealing profound truths about our relationship with God. But when we reach Abraham in Genesis 12 we begin to be in touch with a historical world known to us through the findings of archaeology.

Abraham and his family had names common in the world at that time. Their lifestyle and customs fit with many things we now know about the Middle East around 1800BC. For instance, Abraham bought a field in which was a cave where he could bury his wife Sarah. The method of sale described in Genesis 23 is also known from other documents of the time.

None of this proves that the story of Abraham happened as Genesis describes it. But it makes it unlikely that the story was simply invented many years later.

When we come to the historical books there are certain points at which the Bible's record can be compared with the records of Middle Eastern rulers and other archaeological discoveries. Here are some examples.

Sennacherib was emperor of Assyria from 705 to 681BC. His official records, found by archaeologists in his capital Nineveh, report his siege of Jerusalem in 701, when Hezekiah was king of Judah:

> As to Hezekiah the Jew, he did not submit to my yoke. I laid siege to forty-six of his strong cities, walled forts and countless small villages in the vicinity and conquered them . . . Himself I made a prisoner in Jerusalem, his royal residence, like a bird in a cage . . .

The Bible's account is in 2 Kings 18–19. It is obviously the same event, though 2 Kings 19 also tells how the city was delivered. Sennacherib naturally glossed over the fact

The beginning of Genesis answers profound questions about God, human nature and the way the world is. Later books of the Old Testament chronicle the history of nations, but still from God's point of view.

The Bible's record is frequently confirmed by archaeological findings.

Like all historians, the Old Testament writers interpreted the events they described. Their descriptions are borne out by other sources of the time, though not always with the same interpretation!

that he didn't actually capture Jerusalem. Like any emperor, he wanted to present even his failures and disappointments as successes!

One important reason why Hezekiah was able to hold out against the siege was that he built a tunnel to bring water inside the city walls from the Gihon spring, which was outside. This detail is reported in 2 Kings 20:20.

In 1880 two boys swimming in the Pool of Siloam found their way through a small passage into a tunnel cut in the rock. It was discovered that the tunnel wound its way through 500 metres of limestone to the Gihon spring. And inside the tunnel was a Hebrew inscription from Hezekiah's time, explaining how workmen beginning from each end had met in the middle. You can still wade through this tunnel today.

One hundred and forty-two years after Hezekiah's reign, when the Jews had been in exile in Babylon for half a century, the Persian king Cyrus conquered Babylon and permitted the Jews to return home. This is referred to in Isaiah 40 and 45, and described in Ezra 1. Cyrus' own account is preserved on the Cyrus Cylinder, an inscription written on clay. Referring to the areas from which captive peoples came, he wrote: 'I gathered together all their inhabitants and restored them to their dwellings.' Here again we see the biblical account confirmed.

There are many points where Old Testament history can't be checked with other ancient records. There are still many gaps in our knowledge. And at some points

> *Archaeology can neither prove the Bible nor disprove its claims, for they are about God. But as all its discoveries increase our knowledge of the world in which the Bible was written, so they enable its distinctive religious message to stand out more boldly.*
>
> Alan Millard, archaeologist

the findings of archaeology raise questions about the biblical record rather than confirming it. But there is enough confirmation from other sources to allow us to say that the historical value of the biblical accounts is always to be taken seriously.

Like all historians, the Old Testament writers interpreted the meaning of historical events in the light of what they thought was important. But there is every reason to believe that their historical writings describe real events, not just the creations of their imagination.

Archaeology cannot prove or disprove the Bible's claims about God, but it can provide a background to biblical history.

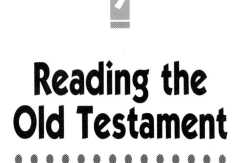

Reading the
Old Testament

● ● ● ● ● ● ● ● ● ● ● ● ●

Not many people begin at Genesis and read straight through to the end of the Old Testament! We need a varied diet. And it isn't always easy to build bridges between words written two or three thousand years ago and our own lives today.

It's a good idea to begin with a book which has plenty of stories, like Genesis. You can read it a chapter at a time, or in longer chunks as you would a novel. Then perhaps read some of the shorter books—the prophecy of Amos or of Micah, the story of Ruth or of Nehemiah. Psalms and Proverbs are two books which can be dipped into a bit at a time, since there is no connecting theme or story between the chapters.

It's helpful to ask certain questions when we are reading a passage. This may seem complicated at first. It's rather like learning to drive. When you begin you think, how will I remember all these different things that I have to do at the same time? But gradually it becomes second nature and you do the right things almost without thinking. With a little practice, we learn

Studying a passage

Let's try out some of these questions on one biblical story—the story of King David's affair with Bathsheba (2 Samuel 11:1-12:14).

What kind of a book?
2 Samuel is one of the historical books which show God working out his purpose through the history of his people. So we shouldn't look for deep meaning in every verse, but see it as part of a longer story of God's dealings with Israel.

What did it mean?
Obviously, the narrative is set in the life of David, about 1000BC. It is tempting for us to see the story as a warning about adultery. That theme is there, but it isn't the main purpose of a historical book. It is part of the story of how God overcame the worst weaknesses of his servants in order to fulfil his purpose.

How can I apply this meaning and put it into practice? Viewed in this way, the story offers us encouragement, and a reason to celebrate God's amazing love. If he could work through David despite his failure, there's hope for us!

What does the New Testament add?
The fact that David was the ancestor of Jesus, God's Messiah, underlines this point about God's love. He never says, 'I told you so', and abandons us to the mess we have created. His love is always looking for fresh ways to achieve his plan to bless the whole of humanity.

naturally to ask the right questions of the passages we read.

What kind of a book is it?

You read a history book in a different way from the instruction manual for a CD player. And different kinds of biblical books need different approaches.

When we read how God shaped the life of someone such as David or Ruth, we can see how he can speak to our own situation. But if we are reading laws in Deuteronomy, we will look for instructions about how to live. In a historical book such as 2 Kings we will look mainly to see how God's purpose for Israel was worked out, and what that might suggest for God's work in the world today.

What did it mean then?

Because the Bible comes from a very different world from our own, we should try to be conscious of the historical context of what we are reading.

If we know, for example, that Amos was prophesying at a time of economic growth and moral decline in the northern kingdom of Israel, shortly before its destruction, we shall make a lot more sense of his message. That's where the introduction to each biblical book which can be found in some Bibles is very helpful.

How can I apply this meaning today?

Sometimes this is easy. A psalm, for example, can immediately suggest ways of praying which are as relevant to us as to an ancient Israelite.

For a passage of the Old Testament to speak to us, we must ask the right questions.

At other times we must tread more carefully. When we read laws which can't be applied directly in our culture we may find a principle underlying the laws which is important for us.

For instance, Deuteronomy 22:8 says: 'When you build a new house, make a parapet around your roof.' This law holds builders responsible for the safety of those who use their buildings. A flat roof without a wall round it was obviously dangerous. The same principle might require that we protect workers from dangerous machinery in factories, or that traffic be barred from streets where children play.

How can I put it into practice?

The Bible is a practical book for people who are aiming to know God better and to do his will. So when we read it we will want to ask, how will this change my understanding of God? How will it help my relationship with him? What difference will it make to the way I live?

What does the New Testament add?

Often the Old Testament doesn't have the last word on a particular topic. So when we read the Old Testament on marriage, for instance, Jesus' words in the Gospels or the teaching of the New Testament letters add important new perspectives. And what the prophets say about God's future plans makes more sense when we discover how those plans are fulfilled in Jesus.

What help can I get?

No one has to struggle with the Bible all alone. In fact, the people who wrote the Old Testament would have found it strange to think that anyone should read these writings on their own. No one in those days had their own books on a shelf at home. They were too difficult and expensive to produce.

The Bible was a book of the community. It was read in the temple or studied in groups. People helped each other to understand and apply it.

Maybe you can study with a group like this. Or you can get Bible reading notes from a church or a bookshop. These will guide you through a variety of biblical books and suggest ways of understanding and putting them into practice.

> **Laws about situations which are specific to Old Testament times can still have underlying principles to guide us today.**

Studying a theme

Sometimes we want to find out what the Old Testament says on a particular subject. Here, for example, is some of its teaching about marriage and families.

◆ **There is instruction.**

Genesis 1:27–28 suggests that God made male and female to be complementary, and that part of their role together is to have children. Genesis 2:18–25 stresses that their relationship is chiefly to provide companionship for each other. When they marry they loosen ties with their parents in order to be wholly committed to each other.

◆ **There are specific laws designed to protect marriage.**

Adultery is forbidden (Exodus 20:14), and a recently married man is excused military service (Deuteronomy 24:5). There are laws too about the respect of children for their parents (Exodus 20:12).

◆ **There are stories about the finding of a marriage partner (Genesis 24) and about love within marriage (Genesis 29–31).**

It is helpful to study the Bible in a group, where people can help each other to understand and apply it.

◆ There are down-to-earth proverbs about attitudes in marriage and the family (Proverbs 5:15–20; 19:13–14; 22:6).

There is a whole section on the qualities of the ideal wife (Proverbs 31:10–31), who runs her own textile business as well as managing her household and caring for her children!

◆ And there is poetry about the passionate love of a young couple (Song of Songs), from both the woman's and the man's point of view.

In ancient Israel, as in many cultures today, the family was not a small unit of two parents and two or three children. It was a wide network of relatives who supported each other through good times and bad. There was always someone to turn to when life was difficult. And single people were also part of these relationships.

The riches of the Old Testament

The Word of God is like a compass, like a map showing the routes, the way to the end. It is food for the soul and without it you are not full, but always hungry.

Thai Christian girl

Such varied material as the Old Testament offers cannot all be applied at face value in the varied cultures of the world today. And the teaching of Jesus and the New Testament revises and enriches it. But it provides the raw materials to guide us. Far from being out of date, its perspective can sometimes challenge the poverty of modern attitudes.

Through myth and poetry, history and legislation, the Old Testament does more than show us the life of a culture that has passed away. It was the Old Testament that formed Jesus' knowledge of God, and it can still speak to us about God today.